D1727863

Freshwater Fishing

John Willis

GONE FISHING

AV2

www.av2books.com

Step 1
Go to **www.av2books.com**

Step 2
Enter this unique code

BRTDVGIVN

Step 3
Explore your interactive eBook!

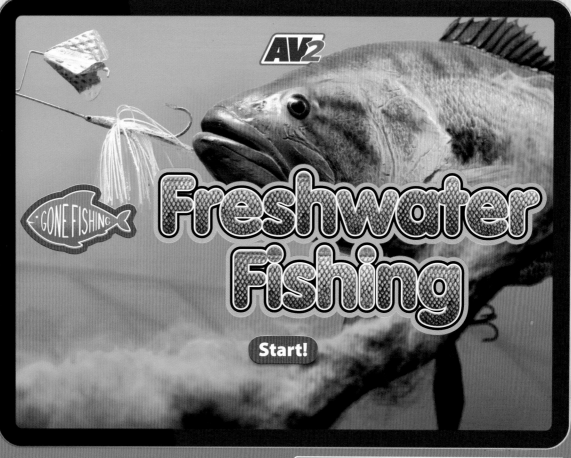

GONE FISHING

Freshwater Fishing

Start!

Your interactive eBook comes with...

AV2 is optimized for use on any device

Read

Audio
Listen to the entire book read aloud

Videos
Watch informative video clips

Weblinks
Gain additional information for research

Try This!
Complete activities and hands-on experiments

Key Words
Study vocabulary, and complete a matching word activity

Quizzes
Test your knowledge

Slideshows
View images and captions

View new titles and product videos at
www.av2books.com

Freshwater Fishing

Contents

Freshwater Fishing

Fresh water is found in lakes, rivers, and streams.

People all over the world enjoy fishing in fresh water.

Lake St. Clair, near Detroit, is known as one of the best **bass** fishing spots in the United States.

Fishing Tools

People use fishing rods to fish in fresh water.

Each rod has a reel and a line with a hook on its end.

Fishers put bait or a lure on the hook.

Freshwater Fish

Fishers use different lures or bait for different fish.

Bass

Bass are some of the most popular freshwater fish.

Many people catch trout, walleye, and catfish as well.

Trout

Walleye

Catfish

Casting

Fishers cast their lines. This puts the hook in the water far away.

When fish bite the bait or lure, fishers pull back on the rod.

Then, they reel in the fish.

Trolling

People can fish from a boat by trolling.

They move the boat slowly and drag a lure behind it.

This makes fish think the lure is alive.

13

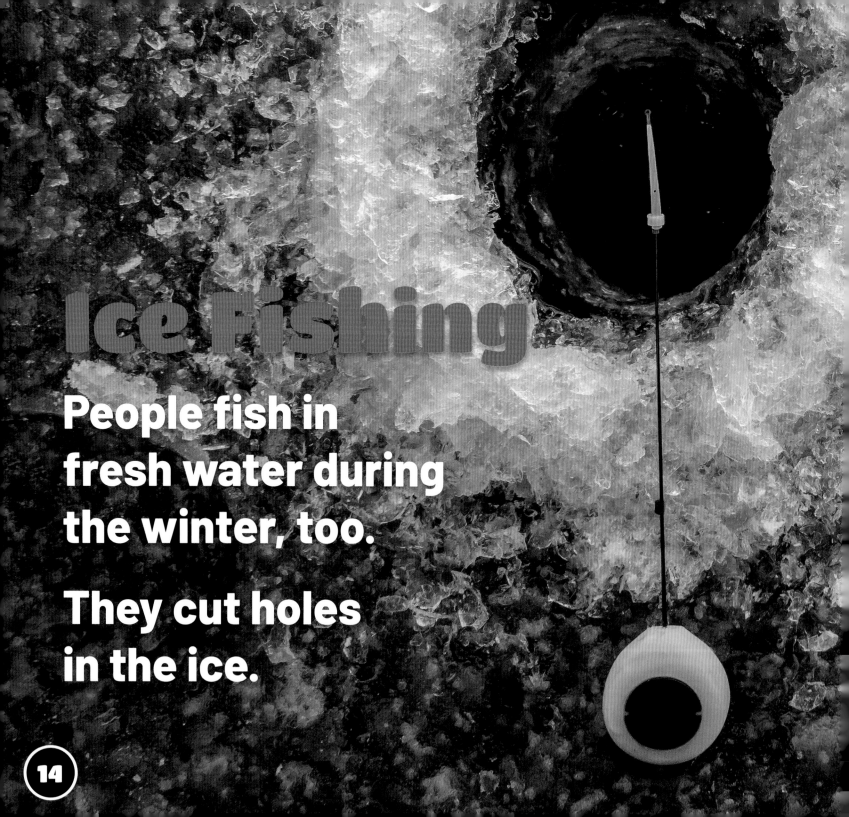

Ice Fishing

People fish in fresh water during the winter, too.

They cut holes in the ice.

Then, they drop their hook and bait into the water.

Freshwater Fishing History

Long ago, people did not fish for fun.

They needed to fish for the food they ate.

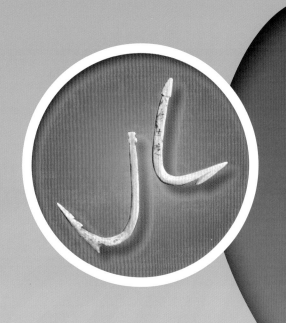

People have **used fishing hooks** for more than **40,000 years.**

Freshwater Fishing Today

Many people still eat freshwater fish today.

Farmers raise freshwater fish such as catfish in ponds.

Then, they catch them using nets.

Fishing Responsibly

It is important to fish responsibly.

People are only allowed to catch a certain amount of fish.

Other people let the fish they catch go.

This makes sure there are enough fish to catch every year.

Freshwater Fishing Facts

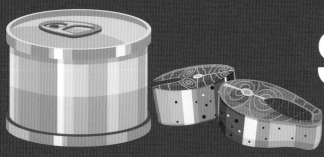

$29.9 billion

In 2016, Americans spent $29.9 billion on freshwater fishing.

Freshwater fishing is the **most popular** way to fish in the United States.

Benefits of Eating Fish

A source of Omega 3 acids.

Heart   Brain   Eyes

Contains Proteins and Vitamin D.

May lower the risk of heart attacks.

Can help brain health.

May help prevent depression.

Can help protect against blindness.

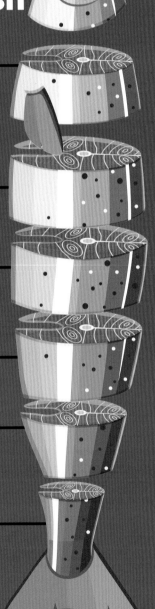

The largest catfish caught in the United States weighed more than **140 pounds. (63 kilograms)**

38.3 million

38.3 million Americans fished in fresh water between 2016 and 2017.

KEY WORDS

Research has shown that as much as 65 percent of all written material published in English is made up of 300 words. These 300 words cannot be taught using pictures or learned by sounding them out. They must be recognized by sight. This book contains 73 common sight words to help young readers improve their reading fluency and comprehension. This book also teaches young readers several important content words, such as proper nouns. These words are paired with pictures to aid in learning and improve understanding.

Page	Sight Words First Appearance	Page	Content Words First Appearance
4	and, found, in, is, rivers, water	4	fishing, fresh water, lakes, streams
5	all, as, known, near, of, one, over, people, the, world	5	bass, Detroit, Lake St. Clair, United States
6	a, each, end, has, its, line, on, to, use, with	6	fishing rods, hook, reel
7	or, put	7	bait, lure
8	different, for	8	fish, fishers
9	are, many, most, some, well	9	catfish, trout, walleye
10	away, far, their, this	12	boat, trolling
11	back, then, they, when	14	holes, ice, ice fishing, winter
12	by, can, from, it, move	18	farmers, ponds
13	makes, think	19	nets
14	cut, too		
15	into		
17	did, food, have, long, more, not, than, years		
18	eat, still, such		
19	them		
20	important, only		
21	enough, every, go, let, other, there		

Published by AV2
350 5th Avenue, 59th Floor New York, NY 10118
Website: www.av2books.com

Copyright ©2021 AV2
All rights reserved. No part of this publication may be reproduced, stored in a retrieval system, or transmitted in any form or by any means, electronic, mechanical, photocopying, recording, or otherwise, without the prior written permission of the publisher.

Library of Congress Control Number: 2019957412

ISBN 978-1-7911-2175-4 (hardcover)
ISBN 978-1-7911-2176-1 (softcover)
ISBN 978-1-7911-2177-8 (multi-user eBook)
ISBN 978-1-7911-2178-5 (single-user eBook)

Printed in Guangzhou, China
1 2 3 4 5 6 7 8 9 0 24 23 22 21 20

032020
100919

Art Director: Terry Paulhus   Project Coordinator: John Willis

Every reasonable effort has been made to trace ownership and to obtain permission to reprint copyright material. The publisher would be pleased to have any errors or omissions brought to its attention so that they may be corrected in subsequent printings.

The publisher acknowledges Alamy, Bridgeman Images, iStock, Minden, and Shutterstock as the primary image supplier for this title.